GO AND OBEY

GOD'S CALL TO ACTION

JOHN W. STANKO

urbanpress

Go and Obey
by John W. Stanko
Copyright © 2019 John W. Stanko

ISBN #

For Worldwide Distribution Printed in the U.S.A.

Urban Press
P.O. Box 8881
Pittsburgh, PA 15221-0881 USA
412.646.2780
www.urbanpress.us

Introduction

I was in Columbus, Ohio in the summer of 2018 listening to Bishop Howard Tillman teach. He was discussing the story of Jesus meeting the woman at the well in John 4. When he got to the part when Jesus told the woman to go and get her husband, Bishop Tillman read it slowly and deliberately, actually pausing for a few seconds after he uttered the words "go and." That pause caused me to consider how often Jesus said the words "go and." While he was still reading, I went to my Bible app on my iPhone and did a search of the New Testament for the combination go and, and quite a few hits came up. Jesus told the rich ruler to "go and" sell what he had, the healed lepers to "go and" show themselves to the priests, the blind man to "go and" wash in the pool, the paralyzed man and the woman caught in adultery to "go and" sin no more, and the apostles to "go and" disciple all nations—just to name a few.

It occurred to me that Jesus was always setting people in motion, directing them to do something. In John 13:17, He said, "Now that you *know* these things, you will be blessed if you *do* them" (emphasis added). James taught, "In the same way, faith by itself, if it is not accompanied by *action*, is dead" (James 2:17, emphasis added). Jesus never said, "Sit, listen, and read, and keep on listening and reading," but unfortunately, that is what some do when they go to church, sing, sit, give, listen, and then go right back into the world in the same spiritual condition as when they came. They may go home and engage in devotional readings throughout the week or watch or listen to a preached message, but they are usually looking for comfort and not confirmation concerning some action steps they are considering. That is not what Jesus had in mind for His followers.

Jesus clearly stated that He expected His disciples to "bear fruit," as we once again look at John's gospel account:

> "I am the true vine, and my Father is the gardener. He cuts off every branch in me that bears no fruit, while every branch that does bear fruit he prunes so that it will be even more fruitful. You are already clean because of the word I have spoken to you. Remain in me, as I also remain in you. No branch can bear fruit by itself; it must remain in the vine. Neither can you bear fruit unless you remain in me.
>
> "I am the vine; you are the branches. If you remain in me and I in you, you will bear much fruit; apart from me you can do nothing. If you do not remain in me, you are like a branch that is thrown away and withers; such branches are picked up, thrown into the fire and burned. If you remain in me and my words remain in you, ask whatever you wish, and it will be done for you. This is to my Father's glory, that you bear much fruit, showing yourselves to be my disciples.
>
> "As the Father has loved me, so have I loved you. Now remain in my love. If you keep my commands, you will remain in my love, just as I have kept my Father's commands and remain in his love. I have told you this so that my joy

may be in you and that your joy may be complete. My command is this: Love each other as I have loved you. Greater love has no one than this: to lay down one's life for one's friends. You are my friends if you do what I command. I no longer call you servants, because a servant does not know his master's business. Instead, I have called you friends, for everything that I learned from my Father I have made known to you. You did not choose me, but I chose you and appointed you so that you might go and bear fruit—fruit that will last—and so that whatever you ask in my name the Father will give you" (John 15:1-16).

This fruit, however it is defined, will probably happen more by going and doing than waiting on the Lord, and I hope this collection of short essays will spur you to action, as we are encouraged to do with one another:

And let us consider how we may spur one another on toward love and good deeds, not giving up meeting together, as some are in the habit of doing, but encouraging one another—and all the more as you see the Day approaching (Hebrews 10:24-25).

Many debate what the "Day" refers to in that passage, but for me, I assume it's the day when my work is done here and I go on to my eternal rest and reward. I want to bear all the fruit I can while I am able, and that means I must be in motion doing something more often than not.

This book examines the connection between the words "go and" to see what we can learn. They were first presented in my weekly online newsletter *The Monday Memo*, and since the response to them was positive every week for five months, I knew a book was in order. When I asked my readers what the title of the book should be, I got back some interesting ideas:

- *What Part of Go Don't You Understand?*
- *The First Two Letters of God's Name Spells GO*
- *God's Bias for Action*
- *Ready, Set, Go!*
- *Go and Don't Look Back*
- *Be God's GO-fer*
- *Go for It!*
- *Go: The Real Message of the Gospel*
- *When God Says 'Go and Do,' You Had Better Go and Do*
- *Go: Responding to God's Call to Action*

I confess: *What Part of Go Don't You Understand?* was my entry in the naming contest and it received a lot of positive feedback. I felt, however, that it was condescending and made it sound like the go-and-obey process was simple and anyone who wasn't going just wasn't being obedient or spiritual. The title I decided on, *Go and Obey: God's Call to Action*, is a bit softer, but still expresses the urgency of finding God's active will and then doing it, whatever the "it" may be.

This is not a long, complex book. Read through the chapters slowly or read the book in one sitting over a few hours. Whatever you choose to do, read with a view toward discerning what God wants you to "go and do."

God is with you and isn't trying to trick or entrap you, so if your heart is to know God's will, His heart is to tell you. I hope this book will enhance in some small way your ability to step out and accomplish God's will for your life. Happy reading!

John W. Stanko
Pittsburgh, PA
February 2019

Chapter 1
Go and
Come Back

When Jesus initiated a dialogue with the woman at the well, she was more interested in discussing religion while debating the doctrine of which mountain was the correct venue for worship. This should sound familiar, for many are still debating that topic and others are in a desperate search for correct dogma about a wide range of life and theological matters. When the woman asked for the living water Jesus mentioned, however, Jesus put her on the right path to establish a relationship with Him that would lead to the water she was seeking:

> Jesus answered, "Everyone who drinks this water will be thirsty again, but whoever drinks the water I give them will never thirst. Indeed, the water I give them will become in them a spring of water welling up to eternal life. The woman said to him, "Sir, give me this water so that I won't get thirsty and have to keep coming here to draw water." He told her, "**Go**, call your husband **and** come back" (John 4:13-16, emphasis added).

This woman did not need correct doctrine; instead,

she needed a correct perspective of her own spiritual condition. She was so used to thinking that if she believed "right," she *was* right and therefore deceived herself into thinking her own spiritual condition and behavior were secondary to doctrine. Because Jesus loved her, He could not leave her in that state of deception.

REALITY

Jesus told the woman to go and get her husband. The woman could have lied and said he wasn't available. She could have gone home, and had the man she was living with come and pretend to be her husband. The beauty of her story is that she told Jesus the truth: She had no husband. It was then that Jesus revealed to her who He truly was, which caused the woman to go back to her village saying, "He told me everything I ever did" (John 4:39). Notice that the truth of her live-in situation did not disqualify her from a relationship with Jesus, but was her actual starting point. Jesus told the woman not only to face the truth, but to face it and then come back to Him.

The woman's reality was the place from which she was to worship. Jesus told her, "Yet a time is coming and has now come when the true worshipers will worship the Father in the Spirit and in truth, for they are the kind of worshipers the Father seeks. God is spirit, and his worshipers must worship in the Spirit and in truth" (John 4:23-24). The truth of worship is not only the truth of who Jesus is but the reality of who each one of us is, not who we are pretending to be, hope to be, or who we think others want us to be.

Jesus is saying to you what He said to the woman: Go, face the reality of who you are, and then come back to Me. That reality is not only your deficiencies, but also

2

your strengths, gifts, and insights He has given you. When will you realize that if you are good enough for God, you should be good enough for yourself? Stop trying to spit shine and polish an image of who you think you need to be to please God and accept who you are. When the woman at the well did that, she found Jesus in a way all those in Israel who were seeking (and thought they were finding) doctrinal truth could not find Him.

A WAY OF LIFE

Jesus was confident that if the woman would follow Him, she would be set free from the brokenness that caused her to be used and abused by men. He was not endorsing her lifestyle or decisions, but He was indicating that none of them had put her on a "disqualified" list when it came to following and worshiping Him. He was not saying, "Get cleaned up and then you can follow Me." He was saying, "Come follow Me and I will help you get cleaned up." There is a big difference. Religion's motto is the first statement, but Jesus came to declare the truth of the second statement.

As you make the journey into self-awareness, which is what Jesus was inviting the woman to do, you will learn that it is your ticket and highway to spiritual growth. It is not a place you visit, but must become a way of life. Face your reality—your fears, weaknesses, gifts, calling, and purpose—and after you do, make sure you come back to Jesus no matter what you find. He already knows what's there, and wants you to know so you can work for Him with a foundation of truth that will always set you free to repeat the process as often as necessary and that process is to *go*, face the truth, *and* then come back to worship Him.

Chapter 2
Go and
Sell Your Possessions

In chapter one, we looked at the story of Jesus' meeting with a woman at a well in John 4, when Jesus ordered her to "go and get your husband." When she confessed that she had no husband, Jesus had what He was after: her need to honestly and openly admit her spiritual condition. In this chapter, we look at an encounter Jesus had with a man who approached Him to ask a question: "Teacher, what good thing must I do to get eternal life?" (Matthew 19:16).

GOOD QUESTIONS

A famous motivational speaker once said that quality questions lead to a quality life. I have found that to be true whenever people are seeking their life purpose, for they must ask questions they have never asked if they want answers they have never heard and received. In the case of this man who came to Jesus, he asked good questions, but those questions led to more truth than he could handle.

Jesus' first response was for the man to keep the commandments. That led to the man's second question, "Which ones?" (Matthew 19:18), to which Jesus answered, "'You shall not murder, you shall not commit adultery, you shall not steal, you shall not give false testimony, honor your

5

father and mother,' and 'love your neighbor as yourself'"
(Matthew 19:19). The man could not leave well enough
alone, however, and he pressed the discussion even further:
"All these I have kept," the young man said. "What do I still
lack?" (Matthew 19:20).

It was then Jesus delivered the explosive answer
that sent the man reeling and retreating to lick his wounds,
desperately seeking to regain his self-righteous equilibri-
um: "If you want to be perfect, **go**, sell your possessions
and give to the poor, and you will have treasure in heaven.
Then come, follow me" (Matthew 19:21, emphasis added).
In Mark's gospel, we are told, "Jesus looked at him, loved
him, and said '**Go and** sell all your possessions' . . ." (Mark
10:21, emphasis added). Because the man kept asking, Jesus
expressed His love by telling the man the truth that his
possessions owned him, and not the other way around.

THE LESSONS

What Jesus told this man did not become the stan-
dard for all people trying to enter the kingdom of God. He
did not say all people had to sell all their possessions, but
Jesus told this man that he had to do so if he was serious
about what he was asking and seeking. Jesus did develop a
lesson that He shared with His disciples from this encounter, and it is this lesson that applies to each of us as we seek
God's will and purpose for our lives: "Truly I tell you, it
is hard for someone who is rich to enter the kingdom of
heaven" (Matthew 19:23).

The reformer John Calvin said, "Man's nature is a
perpetual factory of idols." We can make an idol out of our
looks, ethnic or tribal origin, career, business, relationships
(spouse, kids, grandkids), money, house, or hobbies. Jesus

was helping the man see that while he was keeping all the rules, something else had hold of his heart—and that hold was going to keep him from obtaining what he was seeking to identify.

What has a hold of your heart? Are you keeping all the rules, the commandments, but missing the bigger picture? Are you asking the right questions and if you are, are you prepared for God's honest answers? In the man's case, Jesus was not trying to ruin his life. He loved the man and wanted him to find the life he was seeking, but that life could only be released when he put following Jesus ahead of his business interests.

As we go through this book, I challenge you to ask God to show you what you must do to gain the kind of purposeful, Kingdom-centered life you have expressed an interest in living. Then when He answers—and He will most certainly answer—take steps to reorder your priorities so that God's purpose, and not a counterfeit imposter, is the main focus of your daily life.

Chapter 3
Go and
Show Yourselves

Recently, I had to have a tooth removed that had given me trouble on and off for more than 40 years. While I was glad for the relief, I also mourned the loss of my tooth. Then I had a wound on my nose that would not heal, so I went to the doctor who did not think it was serious, but advised me to cover it for two weeks and come back. When I came back, it had not healed so they performed a biopsy and discovered it was a form of skin cancer called basal cell. I knew this was not to be taken lightly, and I had some anxiety over it until I entrusted it to God's watchful care. I am glad to report the treatment healed my nose. Why do I tell you this? I'm glad you asked; let me explain

LEPROSY

While experiencing these minor physical ailments, I reflected on what it must have been like to have leprosy in biblical times. I had never considered the emotional trauma for someone who witnessed their own flesh being eaten away and then having to endure being an outcast, away from family support systems and care. When I thought of all that, I appreciated even more the significance of Jesus' ministry to those poor souls, who had no hope of a cure until the Heavenly Healer came along. Having set that background, let's look at the account in Luke 17:11-14:

> While He was on the way to Jerusalem, He was passing between Samaria and Galilee. As He entered a village, ten leprous men who stood at a distance met Him; and they raised their voices, saying, "Jesus, Master, have mercy on us!" When He saw them, He said to them, "**Go and** show yourselves to the priests." And as they were going, they were cleansed (emphasis added).

These men, outcasts who were living in caves or mountain regions where they would not have any contact with people, had somehow heard about Jesus. They came to the village, the place where they usually begged for food, perhaps provided by family or people who took pity on them, and had a chance encounter with Jesus. Those ten men, who were a collection of Jews and Samaritans usually divided by ethnic hatred, were joined together by their common human plight and cried out to Jesus for help. True to His nature, Jesus heard their cry for mercy and responded.

GO AND DO SOMETHING

In Luke 5, Jesus healed a leper by touching him, a breathtaking act of compassion, for people did not normally have physical contact with lepers, adding to the lepers' emotional suffering. In the Luke 17 story, Jesus did not touch them or even say, "Thou art healed!" He told them to **go and** show themselves to the priests, which was required by the Law (see Leviticus 14). They went not because they were already healed but because Jesus told them to go while they were still lepers. As they went (not *before* they went or *after* they got to the priests), they were totally, completely, and miraculously healed. They were healed as they walked in obedience. I had never noticed that in the story before writing this.

This story is astounding, for the men had faith in Jesus. They knew they had to report to the priests when healed so the priests could reinstate them to community contact and fellowship. Even though they were *not* yet healed, however, they knew that Jesus would not send them unless they would be healed, so they went—and were healed at some point along the way.

The lessons for us are profound. The lepers acted in faith *before* they saw the evidence or results of their faith. They obeyed their Master and headed off to the priests and got the result they had hoped for while they were on the way. What is God asking you to do that your obedience can then unlock the desired result? Is He telling you to **go and** attend school, to **go and** take a missions trip, to **go and** give money to someone in need, or to **go and** start your ministry, business, orphanage, or medical clinic.

If you respond, "I don't have the resources to do any of that," then think of those ten lepers who had nothing in their power to control except to **go and** obey. As they did, they were healed of a dreaded disease for which there was no cure. As you go, you will find the money, the time, the energy, the wisdom, and the partners to help you with what you cannot do because you did the one thing you could do, and that was **go and** do, and the rest was taken care of. Enjoy the journey and begin thanking God for what He is going to do as you set out in obedience to His word, confident in His ability to guide and provide.

Chapter 4

Go and
Wash in the Pool

Jesus always put people in motion, so to speak, because faith always requires action of some type. In John 9, there is the story of the man born blind, which is one of my favorites. Let's look at this narrative in light of this book's theme to go and obey:

> As he went along, he saw a man blind from birth. His disciples asked him, "Rabbi, who sinned, this man or his parents, that he was born blind?" "Neither this man nor his parents sinned," said Jesus, "but this happened so that the works of God might be displayed in him. As long as it is day, we must do the works of him who sent me. Night is coming, when no one can work. While I am in the world, I am the light of the world." After saying this, he spit on the ground, made some mud with the saliva, and put it on the man's eyes. "**Go**," he told him, "wash in the Pool of Siloam" (this word means "Sent"). So the man *went* and washed, **and** came home seeing (John 9:1-7, emphasis added).

THE PLAYERS

There are three main characters in the first part of

this story, and in the latter part we meet his parents and the Jewish authorities who were offended by Jesus' miracle. Let's break down who the main protagonists were. The first was the blind man, who had never seen in his entire life, a victim of congenital blindness. The second group was made up of Jesus' followers who wanted to debate the reason or source for the man's condition. The third character was Jesus, who wanted to heal the man. The fourth were his parents, who were so intimidated by the Jewish officials that they could not rejoice because of their son's miraculous healing. And the Jewish officials comprised the final group who launched a congressional hearing of sorts to get to the bottom of the dastardly deed performed by healing a blind man on the Sabbath.

The context of this story is Jesus' lesson that He is the light of the world who requires that His disciples do good deeds and fulfill their purpose while they have the chance to do so. Jesus' healing in this case involved the strange act of spitting on the ground, making mud, and then smearing the mud on the man's blind eyes. He then told the man to go and wash in the historic pools of Siloam, built by Hezekiah to provide water in Jerusalem in case the city was ever under siege.

THE LESSONS

Jesus required that the man play a role in his own healing. Jesus told the man to go, something that was not easy for a blind man to do. Perhaps someone led him or maybe he was familiar with the way to the pool. Whatever the case, the man went immediately and obediently, and after he washed, he came back and was healed. The name of the pool literally means "sent" so the man was sent by the Sent One to the pool named Sent to find his healing. Jesus was the start and finish, the Alpha and Omega of the man's recovery, and the same is true for you and me. You should get the idea that Jesus wanted this man to know that he was "sent" by the "Sent one" to a place called "sent."

When people find their purpose, they ask me all the time how they will fulfill their purpose. I had to face the same question in 1991 when I began teaching on purpose. Today, 27 years later, I do so when I write, publish, travel, speak, consult, broadcast, and coach. The One who gave me my purpose is the same One who has helped me fulfill my purpose. The Sent One sent me to you, and tells me to tell you that He is sending you like He sent me. He has been the Alpha and Omega of my purpose—He started it and has helped me achieve it. The same will be true for you.

Now that Jesus has opened your eyes to your purpose and creativity, He will continue to open your eyes, but you must "go and do something." You must **go and** write, paint, rhyme, create, learn, expand, dance, build, give, or travel. You are not to be like some of the characters in John 9 who wanted to debate or judge what Jesus was doing. You must not be like the man's parents who were terrified to embrace the moment. You must be like the blind man who obeyed immediately and, even though he could not see his way forward, found his way. As he did, he found his healing—and then made His way back to Jesus to begin the process all over again. That is your model to follow and as you go, you will find all the resources and strength you need for the journey. Stay behind and you will be like one of those who watched, feared, and even opposed what Jesus was doing when the Sent One sent one to find his healing.

Chapter 5
Go and
Leave Your Life of Sin

In John 8, there is the story of the woman who was caught in adultery. The religious leaders brought her to Jesus for sentencing, hoping to trap Jesus in words or an act contrary to the Law of Moses. Jesus gave the woman instructions to "go and . . .," and it is that encounter that is the focus for this chapter..

SETTING THE SCENE

This story raises a few questions that are impossible to answer but first, let's look at the narrative itself:

At dawn he appeared again in the temple courts, where all the people gathered around him, and he sat down to teach them. The teachers of the law and the Pharisees brought in a woman caught in adultery. They made her stand before the group and said to Jesus, "Teacher, this woman was caught in the act of adultery. In the Law Moses commanded us to stone such women. Now what do you say?" They were using this question as a trap, in order to have a basis for accusing him. But Jesus bent down and started to write on the ground with his finger. When they kept on questioning him, he straightened up and said to them, "Let any one of you who is without sin be the first to throw a stone at her." Again he stooped down and wrote on the ground. At this, those who heard began to go away one at a time, the older ones first, until only Jesus was left, with the woman still standing there. Jesus straightened up and asked her, "Woman, where are they? Has no one condemned you?" "No one, sir," she said. "Then neither do I condemn you," Jesus declared. "**Go** now **and** leave your life of sin" (John 8:1-11, emphasis added).

The questions this story raises are:

1. Why did they only bring the woman and not the man caught in adultery?
2. What was Jesus writing on the ground?
3. Why did the older leaders leave first and then the younger?

We will not take time to speculate on these questions, for we can only surmise and postulate the answers. Instead, let's focus on Jesus' response to the woman's alleged sin.

SIN

When Jesus was left alone with the woman, He said that He would not condemn her and then in essence told her, "Go and stop it!" He did not send her for counseling; He did not lecture her once everyone was gone. He did not remind her of what the Law said. He did not tell her He was disappointed in her. He told her to go and sin no more. What does this tell us?

It tells us that we can too often wallow in our

failures, convinced that we must go through major "recon-struction" before God can use us or even have fellowship with us. This encounter reminds me of Saul's encounter on the Damascus road in Acts 9. God did not beat Saul over the head because of his sin, and his sin was grievous, for he was persecuting believers. The Lord simply told Saul to stop kicking against the goads and then gave him a purpose assignment to the Gentiles.

Perhaps you read this and think I am making light of sin, which of course is terrible and causes repercussions that often affect other people besides the sinner (think of the problems that David's sin caused for his family as one example). Even in David's case, however, God still used and had close fellowship with David. Of course, the best strat-egy to follow is *not* to sin. In case that strategy fails, which it usually does, then you must learn how to run to God when you fail.

Have you allowed your failures or weaknesses, even your sins, to disqualify you from fulfilling your purpose and being productive for God? Yes, get counseling if you need it. By all means, make restitution and ask forgiveness where necessary. Do what you must to get back into the game of life and purpose, so to speak, even if you have to spend time on the disabled list. Jesus was not shocked or scandalized by the woman's sin and we should follow His example by not making sinners pay a higher price for restitution than Jesus would require—or to demand it of ourselves.

Chapter 6
Go and
Throw Out Your Line

This chapter's story comes from the account found in Matthew 17:24-27:

> After Jesus and his disciples arrived in Capernaum, the collectors of the two-drachma temple tax came to Peter and asked, "Doesn't your teacher pay the temple tax?" "Yes, he does," he replied. When Peter came into the house, Jesus was the first to speak. "What do you think, Simon?" he asked. "From whom do the kings of the earth collect duty and taxes—from their own children or from others?" "From others," Peter answered. "Then the children are exempt," Jesus said to him. "But so that we may not cause offense, **go** to the lake **and** throw out your line. Take the first fish you catch; open its mouth and you will find a four-drachma coin. Take it and give it to them for my tax and yours" (emphasis added).

THE BACKGROUND

In Moses' time, each person over the age of 20 was to give an annual half-shekel offering (the equivalent of two Roman drachmas) for the support of the tabernacle (see

Exodus 30:11-16). This practice was obviously still being observed in Jesus' day some 1,500 years later to maintain the Temple. When the tax collectors asked Peter if Jesus paid the tax, he impetuously responded in the affirmative. When he next met Jesus, the Lord raised the issue with Peter, explaining that He was royalty and did not have to pay the tax, which was a subtle reference to the fact that Jesus was the king of Israel.

Peter had made a commitment, however, and Jesus cooperated with Peter's promise to pay the tax. He told Peter to go to the lake and throw out his fishing line. He was to examine the first fish he caught, which would have the coin in its mouth to pay the tax for both men. The story does not indicate Peter did this, but the assumption certainly is that Peter found it to be just as Jesus had promised.

This story follows immediately after Jesus had predicted His death and resurrection, not long after His transfiguration and close to the time when Peter had his "get behind me Satan" encounter with Jesus in Matthew 16. This story is a simple but clear confirmation that Jesus knew what He was talking about. If He could accurately predict that a fish caught on the first try would have money in its mouth, then He was accurate in *everything* He said, which included His prediction of His death and resurrection.

THE LESSONS

There is another aspect to the story worth examining and it is Jesus' cooperation with and tolerance of Peter's less-than-perfect behavior. Peter made a rash statement, but Jesus did not overrule His disciple's commitment to pay. Instead, Jesus agreed to pay on behalf of them both to cover Peter's mistake. I take great comfort from this story, for I too have made many mis-steps in my pursuit of purpose. Some of those mistakes were honest in that I made the best decision with the information I had while desiring to do the will of God. In response to my imperfection, Jesus did not abandon me. He did not revoke my purpose or chastise my efforts.

God is not nearly as short-tempered as we have sometimes made Him out to be. He is not as concerned about us "getting ahead of Him" or "missing Him" as we sometimes are. That reality should free us, not to be rash and cavalier about what we do, but to move forward with our ideas and creativity as we seek to bear fruit for Him. For example, I cannot say that the Lord "told" me to write any of my books. I had ideas, I wrote, and now I am helping others write. There have been times when I threw out a line and found the provision I needed, just in the nick of time, to be creative or purposeful.

Can you imagine the impact it had on Peter when he went down and caught that fish? What a sense of joy and wonder He must have experienced. What a sense of relief that He had the money to do what He had promised to do. Our faith commitments, when realized, are always the most exhilarating experiences in our walk with the Lord. They also become our most meaningful and lasting testimonies. I urge you to trust the Lord and step out to do God's will, no longer afraid that you are overstepping your bounds, but trusting that you are functioning in partnership with your Lord who is for you, not against you, despite your imperfections.

Chapter 7
Go and Make Preparations

In this chapter, let's focus on the account of the disciples preparing for what we know to be the Last Supper, but for them was the traditional Passover meal. This was to be celebrated as a family, but most of the disciples' families were up north in Galilee and they were with Jesus in Jerusalem. I wonder how their absence affected their families? Were they upset? Angry? Understanding? Resentful? That, however, is not our concern, for we want to look at how they made preparations for what they thought was a traditional meal, but instead turned out to be so much more.

THE PREPARATIONS

Then came the day of Unleavened Bread on which the Passover lamb had to be sacrificed. Jesus sent Peter and John, saying, "**Go and** make preparations for us to eat the Passover." "Where do you want us to prepare for it?" they asked. He replied, "As you enter the city, a man carrying a jar of water will meet you. Follow him to the house that he enters, and say to the owner of the house, 'The Teacher asks: Where is the guest room, where I may eat the Passover with my disciples?' He will show you a large room upstairs, all furnished. Make preparations there."They left and found things just as Jesus had told them. So they prepared the Passover (Luke 22:7-13, emphasis added).

The disciples had prepared many Passover meals in the past, so this one was no different, except that they had to find a venue since they were all away from home. Jesus gave them some rather unusual instructions that would enable them to find a place. First, they were to look for a man carrying a water jar, which was highly unusual, for carrying water was women's work. Then they were to follow the man and ask the owner of the home where he entered for permission to hold their celebration there.

Naturally, it all unfolded just as Jesus had instructed them. I have always said that God is a great administrator, able to organize whatever it is He wants to do. The disciples had no idea this upper room even existed until they needed it, and then Jesus directed them out of their need to the exact spot they required. God will do the same for you, for there are unlimited resources out there of which you are unaware. Your role is to listen and then obey, seeing that your need is creating a deeper need—reliance on God for the provision that will help you fulfill God's purpose for your life.

THE REAL LESSON

The more important lesson in the story is the unexpected outcome of what the disciples considered a traditional gathering. This was to be like no other Passover meal since the first one in Egypt, for at this meal, Jesus inaugurated a rite we call communion, the Lord's table, or the Eucharist, which has been repeated countless times for the last 2,000 years.

The disciples' obedience to Jesus' specific and clear directives required faith and mindful obedience, but was not their most important role in the story. Their presence at the dinner enabled them to observe and hear what Jesus did and said, and they went forth from that room and continued to follow His instructions: which were to do what they had just done in remembrance of Him and His imminent sacrifice. They thought they were going to a Passover meal, of which they were familiar, but instead were part of a new practice that would impact the entire world.

That is the kind of expectation we must have as we follow and obey the Lord. We don't know the significance of the missions trips we take, poems we write, businesses we start, or relationships we develop. We may think we understand what we are doing, but there may be much more than what we think. Therefore, we must make the most of every opportunity, not assuming we understand the significance of what we are about to do, especially if we have done it many times before.

I have been to Kenya more than 100 times, but a trip I completed in August of 2018 was special. I probably had the greatest impact I have ever had in my two weeks there. I prepared for the trip, did everything as I had always done it, but something was different and unusual, and it took my breath away. That is what happens when you prepare and trust the Lord, for He is "able to do immeasurably more than all we ask or imagine, according to his power that is at work within us" (Ephesians 3:20).

I urge you to work and prepare for the unexpected with hope that the next time you do it, even if you have done it many times before, you are on the verge of something that will change the world—and if not the world, then at least impact *your* world. It's time for you to go and make preparations.

Chapter 8
Go and
Do Likewise

In this next chapter, let's examine the story of the Good Samaritan, one of Jesus' well-known parables. Jesus told this story in response to a question from an expert in the Law about the Old Testament command to "love your neighbor as yourself." The lawyer wanted to engage Jesus in a debate about who his neighbor was, but Jesus would have none of it. At the end of the story, Jesus asked the expert this question and concluded with this command:

> "Which of these three do you think was a neighbor to the man who fell into the hands of robbers?" The expert in the law replied, "The one who had mercy on him." Jesus told him, "**Go and** do likewise" (Luke 10-36-37, emphasis added).

What can we learn from the lessons in this parable that would be useful in our own lives and quest for purpose?

OVER-SPIRITUAL

I have watched people over the years over-spiritualize Jesus' command to "go and do likewise," and have done it myself. We are waiting on the Lord to lead and guide us to do good deeds, not wanting to get ahead of the

Lord or step out of His will. It is humorous to picture the Lord saying to someone, "**Who** told you to help all those orphans? I wanted you to help 10 but you have helped 100! How dare you? I wanted those other 90 to suffer and maybe even starve. Now I am **angry**!" Or "Who told you to visit the sick in the hospital or minister to those elderly people? I am the boss around here, and I didn't tell you to go. Now I am *really* upset!"

Both of those fictitious scenarios are ludicrous, but that is how we have acted at times, so afraid of getting ahead of the Lord, so fearful of doing the wrong thing that we do **no** thing. I heard a pastor say once that the need is the call. What did he mean? He meant that if you see a situation that requires your help, you should not pray about it or delay. You should address the need, and that may require a significant investment of your time and energy.

Still, you may be wondering, "But if I see the need, where is the Lord in all that? How do I know it's His will to be involved?" Good question; let's try to answer.

NOT EVERYONE SEES

When you see a need, you assume it is so clear that everyone must certainly see it. If they don't do something about it, then they are callous or negligent. That may be true, but in most cases, the others *cannot* see what you see because it's not part of their purpose. When you *go and* see the children suffering or an organization's dysfunction, it's because you are viewing those situations through the eyes of your gifts and purpose. When you see it, it's so you will get involved and educate others as to the need. Even if they aren't stirred to action, however, it doesn't mean you are exempt from doing something. You have seen it and now *you* must do something about it. The need you see then becomes all the call you require—and all the call you are going to get.

Where are you to "go and do likewise" by having mercy on those in need? Is it in your country or outside its borders? Is it in conjunction with another organization or are you to start your own? Is it something other people understand and support, or are you to pioneer the work and lead the way for others to be involved? Is it a one-time need or something that you must do again and again for a few or many?

Jesus was purposely vague in answering the expert, not giving him the specifics of who was his neighbor so there would be no rules to follow, no easy answer to the lawyer's question. The answer for you isn't simple either, and requires you to look for a reason and way to act, not for a reason for inaction. Don't worry so much about getting ahead of the Lord and stop waiting for God to direct your every move. Armed with your go-and-do-likewise attitude, find those who need your help and then do the good deeds you were created to do.

Chapter 9
Go and Learn

When I first started this *Go and Obey* series, I thought I would be finished after a few weeks, but I kept seeing more and more examples of Jesus telling people to go and do something specific. In this chapter, we look at what Jesus said in response to criticism that He was spending too much time with sinners and tax gatherers:

> When the Pharisees saw this, they asked his disciples, "Why does your teacher eat with tax collectors and sinners?" On hearing this, Jesus said, "It is not the healthy who need a doctor, but the sick. But **go and** learn what this means: 'I desire mercy, not sacrifice.' For I have not come to call the righteous, but sinners" (Matthew 9:11-12, emphasis added).

Jesus was telling men who made the study of God's word the work of their adult lives to go and meditate on a verse from Hosea because they did not know what it meant. That should provide a warning to us who believe we are adherents to God's word and who have more resources available to study and understand God's word than any generation in history. We may think we understand something but in reality we do not. Let's look more closely at our need to go and learn more.

The More You Know

When I teach classes on preaching, I give my students this advice: "Whenever you approach a passage of Scripture, no matter how much you have studied it, no matter how much you think you know, you must approach it as if you know nothing at all." Why do I say that? I do so because when we are confident we see everything there is to see about a truth or a passage, we stop looking for more. We are confident, sometimes even smug, that we know all there is to know about it—just like the men Jesus was talking to.

Jesus was talking to men who had memorized the verse He referenced. That had discussed and debated it, and had added much to their collective commentary about its implications for their lives as they served the Lord. They were so sure of their knowledge that they could not see how Jesus' work among sinners was in any way related to the verse from Hosea 6:6: "For I desire mercy, not sacrifice, and acknowledgment of God rather than burnt offerings."

Jesus told the Pharisees they had not "arrived," but were still students in need of study and enlightenment. They knew the Bible but they were missing out on what God was doing through Jesus' public ministry. He is saying the same thing to us today.

Go and Learn

What is it that we may need to go and learn regardless of how long we have known the Lord or the people among whom we live and work? Consider these options:

- If you think you know all there is to know

about who you are or what God wants you to do, you need to go and learn more.

- If you think you know all there is to know about another person and their capabilities, you need to go and learn more.

- If you think you know all there is to know about a Bible story or passage you have studied regularly and taught on repeatedly, you need to go and learn more.

- If you think there is no need for you to learn new skills or gain new knowledge, that you can rely on what you have done in the past to carry you into the future, you need to go and learn more.

- If you think you know the mind of God on politics, justice, mercy, theology, religion, or any other topic, you need to go and learn more.

- If you think you can comment on social media with absolute certainty about **any** matter to correct or lecture someone else and turn them from the error of their ways, you need to go and learn more.

Learning is not something you do for a certain period of life; it is a lifelong pursuit. You are always in need of more wisdom and knowledge so you can be more effective for Him and less dependent on your past, your position, your title, or even your insight. This is the reason I went back to school when I was 57 years of age. This is my motivation to listen to and read as many books as possible. This is my incentive to listen when people give me feedback. I want to "go and learn," and that will be my motto until I run out of strength or die.

Jesus told those who thought they "owned" God that they needed to go and meditate on one verse to find out what it meant. I know I need to do that when I write, preach, or teach. I invite you to join me so that together we can continue to grow and develop to be the masters of our purpose, effective for Him while always striving for more and better. It's always a good time for us to **go and** learn.

Chapter 10
Go and Tell

Let's look at Jesus' words to the man whom He delivered from the torment of a legion of demons for our next *Go and Obey* lesson. After the man was clothed and in his right mind, we read about what happened when Jesus got in the boat to depart:

> As Jesus was getting into the boat, the man who had been demon-possessed begged to go with him. Jesus did not let him, but said, "**Go** home to your own people **and** tell them how much the Lord has done for you, and how he has had mercy on you." So the man went away and began to tell in the Decapolis how much Jesus had done for him. And all the people were amazed (Mark 5:18-20, emphasis added).

Jesus did not allow the man to go with him, but instead told him to go home and tell his family, friends, and neighbors what Jesus had done for him. Let's examine this strategy that sent this man back home to see what we can learn and apply.

The Man Had a Story

We learn this man was from a region known today

as Jordan, but then was a collection of ten cities on the far eastern side of the Roman Empire that were hubs for Greek and Roman culture. This man was a spiritually-oppressed Gentile and Jesus went out of His way to come find the man and set him free. The man was so impacted by what Jesus did that He begged Jesus for permission to accompany Him wherever He was going. Instead, Jesus sent him home to tell his fellow Gentiles what God had done for him.

I can understand why the man wanted to be with Jesus. Hours earlier, he was tormented by a pack of devils that, when released from him, went into 2,000 swine, who immediately went stampeding down a hill to drown in the lake. Can you imagine the stench and mess from 2,000 pig carcasses floating in the Sea of Galilee? The man had a story, however, and Jesus wanted him to spread the word about his miracle, perhaps as a harbinger of the good news that would infect the world after Jesus' departure. The man had a story and Jesus told him to go home and make a spectacle of himself, draw a crowd, and declare what he knew about God's mercy.

YOU HAVE A STORY TOO

You have a story too and you probably have had the same desire as the man had. You want to stay close to Jesus and perhaps have even said, "I just want to be where you are, Lord." That often means being close to Jesus in your devotional life or in church. Jesus basically told the man, "I don't want you to be where I am; I want you to go where I am *not*." The man obeyed, but all we know is that the people were amazed. There are no reports of any from his audience coming the Lord for themselves.

When I say that God wants you to go where He isn't, what comes to mind? Do you think of missions or door-to-door visitation? That may be what God has in mind for you, but that may not be practical or feasible. I know what is possible, and that is to use the technology available to you to tell how much Jesus has done for you. You can write a book, record a testimony, compose a poem, or write and put on a one-person play. Instead of using Facebook to tell people you went to the mall or washed your hair, tell them about God's goodness.

Since I started my publishing company, I have encountered many people who claim God told them to write. Many say they will call me so they can follow through, but most don't. They talk themselves out of it and instead just "stay close to Jesus" in prayer and devotions. That's good but that's not writing a book.

It's interesting that Jesus sent the man home because it was how the man could best maintain his deliverance. You wonder, "How could the man stay free by being apart from Jesus?" Perhaps Jesus had Revelation 12:11 in mind before it was ever written: "They triumphed over him by the blood of the Lamb and by the word of their testimony; they did not love their lives so much as to shrink from death."

Perhaps some of your freedom and deliverance won't happen by staying close to Jesus, but by sharing your testimony? If that's true, then no amount of wishful thinking or spiritually-sounding "I want to be close to the Lord" will do the job. You are going to have to do what the man did: He obeyed Jesus, went home, and told everyone how once he lived with a bunch of devils but God set him free.

Who knows who is desperately waiting to hear your report of what Jesus has done for you. It's time for you to go and tell your story of God's goodness in your life by any and every means at your disposal.

Chapter 11
Go and Be Freed

For this next *Go and Obey* lesson, let's stay in the gospel of Mark to look at the story of the woman who was healed after she touched Jesus' garment. After Jesus inquired as to who had touched Him, we read,

> Then the woman, knowing what had happened to her, came and fell at his feet and, trembling with fear, told him the whole truth. He said to her, "Daughter, your faith has healed you. **Go** in peace **and** be freed from your suffering" (Mark 5:33-34, emphasis added).

Let's look more closely at this fascinating scenario.

FAITH

Faith and healing are a mystery as to their connection. You probably know someone who has been accused of not receiving something, maybe even a healing, because he or she did not have enough faith. Perhaps that has happened to you. That accusation can sting and leave a wound for a long time, causing people to be disappointed and disgruntled with the Lord and with other believers, or blaming themselves for their situation.

I know God heals. I have seen it happen and prayed

to cause it to happen. I can't answer why He doesn't always heal, except to say that we would probably begin to put our trust in how the healing happened, or in the format or formula of the healing prayer. We would then be able to turn God's power off and on like a light switch, and soon we would be impressed with our own ability. Because of our desire to control God or tendency to reduce Him to someone we can more easily understand, we would put our trust in our faith instead of in God.

This is perhaps why Jesus healed in a variety of ways. One time He spit and made mud. Another time, He spoke or laid His hands on someone. If He would have healed in the same manner, we would have made a ritual of the process, establishing rules and regulations for healing.

BE FREED

The woman touched Jesus while He was on His way to visit the sick daughter of the synagogue leader. This story shows there is neither a limit to Jesus' power nor is He overwhelmed by human need because He came to overcome sin and death, our last enemy. We will all die unless the Lord returns, and we will die from some ailment or simply of old age. Hebrews 11:13 tell us, "All these people were still living by faith when they died. They did not receive the things promised; they only saw them and welcomed them from a distance, admitting that they were foreigners and strangers on earth." I have decided I would rather die in faith than live in fear or presumption, so I will do what the woman did in as many situations as I can. She did not allow her history or the hopelessness of her situation to prevent her from pressing forward and trusting God.

Right now, I am believing God for finances—again. It seems like this has been the struggle of my adult life. God has provided, but there are long stretches where I second-guess myself and cry out, "God, where are You?" Regardless of how often this has happened, I am following the woman's example. I am pressing through the crowd of my doubt, refusing to be defined by my past experience while straining and striving to be freed. I live in reality but I know the Lord's love and power, and I refuse to give up or give in to my lack.

Perhaps you are struggling again with pain or suffering, whether it be emotional or physical. I can only encourage you to press on and press through. I know the Lord wants you to be free and I cannot explain the reasons why you are not, but don't give up. Can you imagine the joy this woman had when she realized the dream of wholeness after a life of misery? That is the same joy you will have when you touch Him and receive what you believed for, even when it seemed beyond your reach or His desire to perform.

Chapter 12
Go and
See

In this chapter, let's look at the story of Jesus feeding the multitudes with five loaves and two fish. Here is the context for the event:

By this time it was late in the day, so his disciples came to him. "This is a remote place," they said, "and it's already very late. Send the people away so that they can go to the surrounding country-side and villages and buy themselves something to eat." But he answered, "You give them something to eat." They said to him, "That would take more than half a year's wages! Are we to go and spend that much on bread and give it to them to eat?" "How many loaves do you have?" he asked. "**Go and** see." When they found out, they said, "Five—and two fish." Then Jesus directed them to have all the people sit down in groups on the green grass. So they sat down in groups of hundreds and fifties. Taking the five loaves and the two fish and looking up to heaven, he gave thanks and broke the loaves. Then he gave them to his disciples to distribute to the people. He also divided the two fish among them all. They all ate and were satisfied, and the disciples picked up twelve basketfuls of broken pieces of bread and fish. The number of the men who had eaten was five thousand (Mark 6:35-44).

What can we learn from this latest command that involved the word *go*?

REALITY

Walking in faith never requires you to ignore reality. The disciples faced the reality that it was getting late and the huge crowd was hungry after a day of listening to Jesus. The problem was they assumed they did not have the resources to feed the people, so they brought the problem to Jesus and outlined the options: send the people home or spend a lot of money they did not have on a picnic lunch.

The disciples did not need money or a dismissal prayer; they needed a new way of thinking. Jesus presented them with a new thought—they already had enough to meet all the needs of the people, with some left over. They had never considered that possibility and therefore had no faith for anything beyond what they could see. Jesus wanted them to see what they had, but then also see that they had enough. They had all they needed to do what God wanted them to do. They simply needed to think differently and exercise faith.

A NEW REALITY

Years ago, I was complaining to the Lord that I had no money for Christmas presents for my friends. I was broke—or so I thought. Then I looked at my magnificent library filled with books I no longer read or needed. I prayed and then picked out a book I thought each friend needed to read and would enjoy. They were all blessed with their book gift, but the point is I already had all I needed for the gifts. I only needed to think new thoughts and change my perspective from lack to abundance.

On another occasion, I was telling the Lord I had no resources to participate in a special church offering. It was then that I thought of my coin collection, which I promptly sold and gave the proceeds in the offering. I had what I needed. I only needed to think new thoughts.

Just a few minutes ago, I was asked to conduct an interview with someone and I needed to send them a link to complete a profile. Money is tight and I didn't want to spend what I had on the profile. Then I looked through my online files and found an unused profile I didn't know I had. I didn't need another profile. I only needed to think new thoughts and not assume there was only one way for me to do what I was asked to do.

YOUR REALITY

Perhaps Jesus is telling you to go and see what you have in your house, mind, experience, or some other place, not to highlight your lack, but to point out that you have more than you thought if you apply faith to it, like Abraham did:

> Without weakening in his faith, he faced the fact that his body was as good as dead—since he was about a hundred years old—and that Sarah's womb was also dead. Yet he did not waver through unbelief regarding the promise of God, but was strengthened in his faith and gave glory to God, being fully persuaded that

God had power to do what he had promised (Romans 4:19-21).

Abraham faced reality, but then faced the more important reality of God's promise. Without denying reality of his lack, he was strengthened in his faith when He focused on God and the Lord provided. Ask God to open your eyes to the reality of what you already have that He can use for His purpose. Then ask Him to give you new thoughts about what you have and don't have, and see if your new thoughts will allow you to re-evaluate your hesitancy to do something for the Lord. You may have your own loaves and fish that you thought were inadequate, but with new thinking you will see as adequate for the task at hand.

Chapter 13

Go and
You Will Be Told

In this next installment of our *Go and Obey* study, we look at the Apostle Paul's encounter with the Lord when he was Saul "still breathing out murderous threats against the Lord's disciples" (Acts 9:1). It surprises me that the Lord appeared to Saul not to rebuke him but to reveal Saul's purpose, which was to take the gospel to the Gentiles. We read this account of Saul's Damascus-road experience:

> As he neared Damascus on his journey, suddenly a light from heaven flashed around him. He fell to the ground and heard a voice say to him, "Saul, Saul, why do you persecute me?" "Who are you, Lord?" Saul asked. "I am Jesus, whom you are persecuting," he replied. "Now get up and **go** into the city, **and** you will be told what you must do" (Acts 9:3-5).

If I were the Lord, I would have chastised him for his bigotry and cruelty in persecuting the Lord's followers. God seemed more concerned with revealing Saul's purpose than his sin, and spoke to him about what he was created to do.

TWO ACCOUNTS

Luke's account in Acts seems to indicate that the

Lord said little to Saul directly, but rather told him he would receive his marching orders from someone in the city where he was heading. Saul had to go and would receive more information on a need-to-know basis. In Acts 26, Paul gave this account of the story 20 years after his encounter with the Lord in Acts 9:

> "Then I asked, 'Who are you, Lord?' 'I am Jesus, whom you are persecuting,' the Lord replied. 'Now get up and stand on your feet. I have appeared to you to appoint you as a servant and as a witness of what you have seen and will see of me. I will rescue you from your own people and from the Gentiles. I am sending you to them to open their eyes and turn them from darkness to light, and from the power of Satan to God, so that they may receive forgiveness of sins and a place among those who are sanctified by faith in me'" (Acts 26:15-19).

The narrative in Acts 26 indicates the Lord said much more than what was originally reported in Acts 9, and there is a simple explanation for this. In Paul's mind, the Lord spoke to him through His servant Ananias, so therefore it didn't matter if Paul reported that the Lord said it or Ananias said it. To Paul, it was one and the same. By the way, Ananias also had a "go and obey" moment when he went to visit Saul as Luke described: "But the Lord said to Ananias, "**Go**! This man is my chosen instrument to proclaim my name to the Gentiles and their kings and to the people of Israel. I will show him how much he must suffer for my name'" (Acts 9:15-16, emphasis added).

LESSONS

Here are some lessons to consider from this *Go and Obey* story.

1. Sometimes we must go and then we will get more information of what to do. Usually, we want the information before we go.
2. God reveals purpose in His time, but when He does, it is often an event that leaves us shaken and moved, requiring time to sort things out.
3. While it is good to hear from the Lord, it is also easier to ignore His voice. Thus, He sends His servants to tell us what He wants us to do.
4. When His servants speak, it is really God who has spoken.
5. The light of purpose can be so bright that it can disorient us, creating our need for people to take us by the hand and guide us.

It is commendable if you are thinking, "I want and need to hear from the Lord," but then you must not box God in as to how He will speak to you. He will use other people, your curiosities, and life circumstances, among other things, to reveal His purpose. You must have faith He is not trying to trick or mislead you, and then once you hear, you must go and obey. Once you get up and go, God will give you more information and clarity, but only if you have a go-and-obey attitude. When you do, God is on the journey with you, and you will have everything you need to carry out His purpose for your life.

Chapter 14
Go and
Take Possession

In 2014, I resigned a ministry position at my church after experiencing five years of success. It was my main source of income and I enjoyed the people and the work—and I think they enjoyed me. I was 64 years old, but I had an idea to start a publishing company to give people without access to editing and publishing services a chance to share their stories. People in publishing at the time advised me not to do it, for publishing was in flux and unstable. I heard them but I knew what I needed to do; I had to take possession of what the Lord had showed me.

In this next installment with a *Go and Obey* theme, let's look at what the Lord told Moses in Deuteronomy 1:8: "See, I have given you this land. **Go** in **and** take possession of the land the LORD swore he would give to your fathers—to Abraham, Isaac and Jacob—and to their descendants after them" (emphasis added) and apply it to our walk of purpose.

GO IN

When the Lord spoke to Moses, the people had a promise that God would give them the Land. The people sent out spies to survey their territory but unfortunately, those spies brought back a negative report. The people believed the report and not the promise of God. Therefore,

God had them wander in the Wilderness until all those who had believed the report were gone and a new generation had taken their place.

I felt I was at a similar place in 2014. I had seen the Promised Land, heard the negative report of those who had seen that Land, and had to decide what I was going to do and "whose report I would believe," as the song says. I opted not to listen and entered in to take possession of Urban Press and the rest is history. To date, I have published or re-published 42 of my own books and produced another 45 book projects for other people. My son is in the business with me, and we have partnered with many first-time authors to help them realize their publishing dreams.

When I made the decision to leave my church position, I woke up at 2:30 the next morning and said to myself, "What have I done?" I did the math and then went back to bed, refusing to give in to the fear of the unknown. The summer of 2018 was the leanest time our company has had, but God has sustained us, and we are about to release or get started on many new projects. It's been great fun.

AND YOU?

Is it time for you to go and take possession of something God has promised you? Maybe it's a business or perhaps it's a ministry, a college degree, a missions trip, learning a new language, or a book, music, or some other creative project becoming a reality. This is not the time to wait, pray, seek confirmation, or procrastinate. It's time to go and take possession. That isn't a super-spiritual act, but one that is divinely practical. If it's a degree, you enroll and go to class. If it's a book, you write it. If it's a business, you incorporate. If it's missions, you take a trip.

The Lord did not transport the people into the Promised Land. They had to walk in. While on their way, they had to eat, sleep, and do all the other things humans do to stay alive. The journey was hot and the days long. That is what it means to go and take possession of what God has promised. That is what you will have to do.

Have you been waiting on the Lord to do what only you can do? Then it's time to get up and get going. When we produce a book, we do it one page at a time until it is finished and then we do another one. There is nothing glamorous about the process, but it is exhilarating to see the finished product(s). The same will be true for you and your promised land. Face your fears, go find the information and resources you need, and then take possession of your land of milk and honey. As you do, I know you will have the same joy I have as you step out and into what is in your heart to do.

Chapter 15

Go and See #2

Up to this point in *Go and Obey*, each of the commands to go and do something has been issued by the Lord. In this chapter, we look at an order that came from a human agent, this time Jacob, Joseph's father. We know Joseph was Jacob's favorite son, so he kept him close to home while the other sons were out tending the herds. The other brothers hated Joseph and Jacob miscalculated the depth of their hatred, so he naively sent Joseph on a reconnaissance mission to check on how the brothers were doing: "'**Go and** see if your brothers are safe and if the flock is all right; then come back and tell me.' So his father sent him on his way from Hebron Valley" (Genesis 37:14a).

Little did Joseph and Jacob know that this would be the last time they would see each other for 22 years. Joseph found his brothers but never got to bring back a report because they sold him into slavery, then sealed their crime with a lie that he had been attacked and killed by a wild animal.

GOD WAS INVOLVED

There is an interesting twist to the story found in the verses immediately following Jacob's commissioning:

Joseph arrived at Shechem and was wandering around in the country when a man saw him and asked him, "What are you looking for?" "I am looking for my brothers, who are taking care of their flock," he answered. "Can you tell me where they are?" The man said, "They have already left. I heard them say that they were going to Dothan." So Joseph went after his brothers and found them at Dothan (Genesis 37:14b-17).

Who was this man who helped guide Joseph to his fate at the hands of his brothers? We don't know, but without him, Joseph would not have found his brothers. God used the man to ensure that Joseph would get to Egypt and carry out God's plan, as Joseph later acknowledged: "Don't be afraid; I can't put myself in the place of God. You plotted evil against me, but God turned it into good, in order to preserve the lives of many people who are alive today because of what happened" (Genesis 50:19b-20). The psalmist corroborated Joseph's perspective when he wrote,

The Lord sent famine to their country and took away all their food. But he sent a man ahead of them, Joseph, who had been sold as a slave. His feet were kept in chains, and an iron collar was around his neck until what he had predicted came true. The word of the Lord proved him right (Psalm 105:16-19).

RESTING IN HIM

Your life may have been changed forever by a chance meeting, an accident, or an unexpected catastrophe or setback, and you have reflected on that event, wondering "what if" it had never happened. You may still be in the midst of processing the consequences, so the full result has not ripened or appeared for the event to make sense. That is where faith comes in. I once read that the *less* we feel or understand, the *more* we should trust. If your life doesn't make sense, if there was an event you considered routine that turned into a life-changer, then it's time to trust God all the more.

I have been reflecting lately on the many life disappointments I have had in ministry. It seems most of what I have done or begun has not ended the way I had hoped, and I have been facing the reality that I have a broken heart where ministry is concerned. I am not sharing that for sympathy, but it is a reality, and I find myself often declaring, "Lord, I trust You, I trust You." I am speaking the truth, for I do trust Him, but that truth cannot gloss over or anesthetize the pain that is there. I look back and see my times when I went to find my brothers, only to be sent off in a direction I did not anticipate, and I feel like I am still waiting for the outcome, resolution, and understanding, which may not come before I pass into God's presence.

I am resting in God these days and not my own perspective, for my insight is limited, and as Joseph said, "I can't put myself in the place of God." I am trusting the Lord that my path is the one He ordained, even when I lack His understanding of the end result. I invite you to join me as we follow in the steps of Joseph to walk out our lives, trusting that what we have often declared is really the truth: The Lord reigns.

Chapter 16
Go and Ask

In late 2018, I finished editing the revisions on my second book I first penned in 1997, I *Wrote This Book on Purpose . . . So You Can Know Yours.* This expanded edition includes seven PurposeCoach sessions not in the original version. In one of those sessions, I discussed the importance of asking good questions to find good answers. That made me think of this week's verse, which we have already looked at in chapter 13: "The Lord told him, "**Go** to the house of Judas on Straight Street **and** ask for a man from Tarsus named Saul, for he is praying" (Acts 9:11, emphasis added).

The Lord gave this command to a man named Ananias and the man who was praying was Saul, who later became known as Paul. Let's re-examine this *Go and Obey* encounter that both men had with the Lord to see what we can learn and apply to our lives.

MORE INFORMATION

The Lord and Ananias went back and forth about this assignment:

> "In a vision he has seen a man named Ananias come and place his hands on him to restore his

sight." "Lord," Ananias answered, "I have heard many reports about this man and all the harm he has done to your holy people in Jerusalem. And he has come here with authority from the chief priests to arrest all who call on your name." But the Lord said to Ananias, "Go! This man is my chosen instrument to proclaim my name to the Gentiles and their kings and to the people of Israel. I will show him how much he must suffer for my name" (Acts 9:12-16).

Ananias did not have enough information after God's command, so in essence, he asked a question for clarification: "Are you sure, Lord, You want me to go? I have heard that this Saul is a dangerous man!" The Lord let Ananias know the purpose He had for Saul, which gave Ananias confidence for his own safety. Notice that the Lord had shown Saul a man was going to pray and heal him from his blindness.

LESSONS

What can we learn from these few verses?

1. The Lord was not offended when Ananias asked for clarification.

2. While both men had a supernatural encounter with God, neither one of them could be fully obedient without the help of the other.

3. Saul was praying and waiting for Ananias to come and set him free.

4. Ananias was given the specifics of where Saul was, but he had never met him, so he had to ask for him by name.

There are people waiting for you to fulfill your purpose. They cannot move on because God has created a partnership between their need and what you have in your possession to meet that need. Your procrastination or hesitation causes them to continue in their situation because you have the key to open their locked door of opportunity, freedom, or understanding. Those people waiting may be across the street, across your town, or across the globe. Your job is to find them. God will give you the specifics but you must "go and ask" for the opportunity that God has assigned you. That may include clarification of how you are to proceed.

That means you must have faith that you have heard from the Lord. Then you must get up and go, trusting it will be as God described when you get there. There may be some perceived danger in what you are called to do, which doesn't disqualify what you heard, for God knows more about the circumstances than you do. That only adds to the faith element you need to succeed.

I encourage you to ask all the questions you need about what you are to do, but by all means get busy *doing* it. People's lives hang in the balance, so you must write your book, make your trip, start your business, or do whatever else you need so you can "go and ask" for the opportunity for which you have prepared. When you go and return, I promise you will have a testimony of how God used you as His agent to set someone free who was waiting for you to come, but didn't know when you would arrive. Don't make them wait any longer.

Chapter 17
Go and
[Give a] Report

For our next lesson in the *Go and Obey* series, let's look at Isaiah 21:6: "***Go***, post a lookout **and** have him report what he sees. When he sees chariots with teams of horses, riders on donkeys or riders on camels, let him be alert, fully alert." The Lord was sending His word to Israel through the mouth of a lookout and He is still doing the same thing today. Let's examine that in the context of your life purpose.

The Lookout Revisited

In Ezekiel 33:7-9, the Lord warned His prophet about not sharing what he saw:

> "Son of man, I have made you a watchman for the people of Israel; so hear the word I speak and give them warning from me. When I say to the wicked, 'You wicked person, you will surely die,' and you do not speak out to dissuade them from their ways, that wicked person will die for their sin, and I will hold you accountable for their blood. But if you do warn the wicked person to turn from their ways and they do not do so, they will die for their sin, though you yourself will be saved."

Ezekiel could not afford to assume that everyone saw or heard what he did. He had to express what he saw—in a sense express who he was—or God would hold him accountable for not sharing his insight. Many people apply this concept only to the prophetic ministry, but it has larger implications. You are also a watchman for God's people in the purpose God has assigned you, and God wants you to feel the same pressure and urgency Ezekiel felt as you express it.

Your Unique Insight

Your purpose causes you to see the world as no one else sees it. What you see is so clear and natural, however, you believe that everyone must see it, and if they are not acting on it, they must be disobedient, lazy, or just plain stupid. What you misunderstand is that your view of the world is unique to who God made you to be. If you don't express what you see through art, the written word, starting a business that meets a need, or some other creative expression, you are depriving the world of a contribution no one else can make that emanates from your unique perspective on life and the people around you.

My purpose is to create order out of chaos without control. When I look at a person or a situation, I see the potential and quite often it is so clear to me that I wonder why others don't respond. They don't react as I do because they can't see it; only I can see it. My job is then to find a way to share what I see or else it won't ever have a chance to be seen by others. I do so "without control," for my job is to convince people of the rightness of what I see, not force them to accept my perspective and act.

When you walk into a room and see hurting people,

you can get angry that no one is helping them because their pain is so obvious to you. Have you ever considered that the others cannot see their pain, and you are the one to point out the pain and the one to do something about it? When you say, "Someone should do something about this or that," have you considered that no one is doing anything because they cannot see the need or don't feel what you feel? Have you further considered that *you* are the *someone* who needs to do *something*?

God is holding you accountable to help others according to the gifts and insight He has given you. Stop complaining that others aren't doing something about your burden and do something yourself. It's time you take your place on the wall and tell the people what you see, however you are wired to communicate that. When you do, you will begin to see that God has designed you to be His special envoy to the world with a message and a mode of delivery found only in you. If you don't respond to what you see when you stand on the wall, then God's cause will be hindered and the people will never have what only you can provide. What's more, you will be held accountable for what you have not done.

Chapter 18
Go and Stay Near

As we continue the *Go and Obey* theme, let's look at the story of Philip and the Ethiopian eunuch:

> Now an angel of the Lord said to Philip, "Go south to the road—the desert road—that goes down from Jerusalem to Gaza." So he started out, and on his way he met an Ethiopian eunuch, an important official in charge of all the treasury of the Kandake (which means "queen of the Ethiopians"). This man had gone to Jerusalem to worship, and on his way home was sitting in his chariot reading the Book of Isaiah the prophet. The Spirit told Philip, "**Go** to that chariot **and** stay near it" (Acts 8:26-29).

Here are some things that stand out to me from the story of this encounter.

THINGS TO THINK ABOUT

1. The angel of the Lord and the Spirit (who seem to be one and the same) spoke to Philip. This was not an extraordinary event, but seemed to be normal in the life of Philip. Is it normal in your life? If not, why not? Do

you even believe this is possible or normal for the Spirit of the Lord to speak to you?

2. The Lord spoke to Philip regarding his purpose (evangelism) and not some random act of kindness. God will speak to you about your purpose as well. You should expect exceptional guidance where your purpose is concerned.

3. Philip received specific, detailed instructions about what he was to do—what road he was to travel and who he was to meet. It turned out exactly as he was told.

4. Philip did not receive specific, detailed instructions about what he was to do once he got there. That only came once he obeyed and went. You may be waiting for information that is not forthcoming. God may direct you to go and you find out what you are to do once you arrive—not before.

5. Once Philip obeyed and got near the chariot, the Spirit did not tell him what to do. He had to come to his own conclusion of the right course of action. He got so close to the chariot that he could hear, and once he heard, then he initiated contact with the eunuch. You may be waiting for specific instructions that will never come, for you are expected to use your brain and reasoning ability to deduce what God wants you to do.

6. Philip did not have to exert much energy

to find the expression for his purpose, but he had to exert great energy to fulfill it. The Lord spoke to him—that was the easy part—but then he had to travel by foot to meet the eunuch and travel some distance from his home to find the target for his purpose expression. You will work in your purpose, not necessarily to find your purpose but to fulfill it. God wants you to know, but then God expects you to "walk" down the desert road He shows you, not worry about how far away from home it is taking you, and then apply your creativity to what you see and hear.

We looked in the last chapter at how you will see things in your purpose that no one else sees. It is easy to assume everyone sees what you see, but they don't, because they aren't wired like you are. The same is true for what you hear. Others would have heard the eunuch and not known what to do, but Philip knew because it involved his purpose. It was the same with Nehemiah when he heard the report of how bad the conditions were in Jerusalem. Others heard the report, but only Nehemiah was moved to action. When you hear things that pertain to your purpose, you will be moved while others have no idea what's happening. If you expect them to move as you do, you will be disappointed or miss your opportunity to serve the Lord.

PERSONAL EXAMS

I can't say God has spoken to me to write any of my books. I am a writer, I have ideas, so I conclude that I am to act on those ideas, without waiting for a sign from heaven.

In fact, signs are for unbelievers, not those who have faith: "A wicked and adulterous generation looks for a sign, but none will be given it except the sign of Jonah" (Matthew 16:4). The sign of Jonah was Jesus' resurrection and that certainly did not convince the unbelievers who were set against Jesus' and His ministry. A sign is no guarantee of obedience; only a heart set on doing God's will is.

I have done a lot of work in Africa, but I cannot say God has always directed my work. He has directed me to go, and I find what I am to do once I *Go and Obey*. If I stay near to my friends there through social media and then make personal visits, my days are full of purposeful activity that is fulfilling and joyful. What's more, I seldom leave Africa before I schedule my next visit. How do I know if I have chosen the right date to return? I don't, but I make my choice and count on God to show me if I am not supposed to go. In most cases, I end up returning on the dates I have chosen. I choose the dates in faith, return in faith, and then carry out my creative purpose while there in faith.

Where or to whom does God want you to go and stay near? You go in faith and only then will you know what else you are to do. When you hear it, you will know it, but you have to act with the same faith that caused you to obey and go in the first place. This should help you de-mystify the concept of obedience, for while the Lord may initiate your good deeds, you will have to decide when and how to fulfill them. The key is to go and then stay near the Lord, just as Philip did. Don't worry, God's not trying to trick you. He wants you to be fruitful, so you can go and do in the freedom you have in Christ.

Chapter 19
Go and
See the Land

We go back to the Old Testament for this chapter's lesson in the *Go and Obey* series. In Numbers, the Lord spoke to Moses as he was about to die:

> "*Go* up this mountain in the Abarim Range **and** see the land I have given the Israelites. After you have seen it, you too will be gathered to your people, as your brother Aaron was, for when the community rebelled at the waters in the Desert of Zin, both of you disobeyed my command to honor me as holy before their eyes." (These were the waters of Meribah Kadesh, in the Desert of Zin) (Numbers 27:12-14).

This story is a mix of human failure and God's grace, so let's examine it more closely to see what we can learn that will help us in our pursuit of purpose and productivity.

THE FAILURE

In Numbers 20, we read why Moses was not permitted to enter the Promised Land with his people:

> So Moses took the staff from the Lord's presence, just as he commanded him. He and Aaron gathered the assembly together in front of the

rock and Moses said to them, "Listen, you rebels, must we bring you water out of this rock?" Then Moses raised his arm and struck the rock twice with his staff. Water gushed out, and the community and their livestock drank. But the Lord said to Moses and Aaron, "Because you did not trust in me enough to honor me as holy in the sight of the Israelites, you will not bring this community into the land I give them" (Numbers 20:9-12).

What was so wrong with what Moses did when he struck the rock? The short version is that the Lord told Moses to speak to the rock and water would come forth. Instead, Moses struck the rock, which we learn later was Christ Himself: "They all ate the same spiritual food and drank the same spiritual drink; for they drank from the spiritual rock that accompanied them, and that rock was Christ" (1 Corinthians 10:3-4). Moses made it appear that God was angry (He was not), and that it was Moses, through his act of striking the rock, who was the one bringing the water forth. For this misrepresentation of God's intent at a time in his life when Moses knew better, he was barred from entering the Land.

THE GRACE

God did not completely banish Moses, but instead allowed him to see the land he was unable to enter, which was an act of God's grace:

All these people were still living by faith when they died. They did not receive the things promised; they only saw them and welcomed them from a distance, admitting that they were foreigners and strangers on earth. People who say such things show that they are looking for a country of their own. If they had been thinking of the country they had left, they would have had opportunity to return. Instead, they were longing for a better country—a heavenly one. Therefore God is not ashamed to be called their God, for he has prepared a city for them (Hebrews 11:13-16).

When Moses saw the land, he welcomed the promise of God and in a sense, he entered into the joy of the Promised Land as if he was actually in it. It didn't stop there, however, for centuries later, he paid another visit to a mountain in that same land, this time to encourage and strengthen Jesus: "Two men, Moses and Elijah, appeared in glorious splendor, talking with Jesus. They spoke about his departure, which he was about to bring to fulfillment at Jerusalem" (Luke 9:30-31). Moses came back to see the most important promise of God, which was not a physical land, but a spiritual restoration to be accomplished through Christ's death and resurrection. Moses' failure could not stop God's grace when he was alive or even after he was gone.

THE LESSONS

What is God revealing to you? Can you receive it in faith and thank Him for it, even though it has not come to pass? I have written a verse-by-verse commentary on the entire New Testament, and it has sold very few copies. It has been on my website for years, free of charge, and I don't know how many people in the world have accessed it. They are now part of a *Live the Word* commentary series, and are presented in a devotional format not only to help people understand the Word, but also to help them apply the lessons to daily life. Why did I produce it (the project took me nine years) and why do I take pains to publish it (requiring another five years at my own expense)? I do so because one day, perhaps after I am gone, God can and will use those commentaries. I have seen the promise and welcomed it from afar, and in a sense, my books are a gift to God to use (or not) as He sees fit.

God has probably already taken you up to a high place to see your Promised Land. I encourage you to enjoy and savor the view, but realize it is not just to be a spiritual experience. It is a reality to be cherished now and in the age to come.

Chapter 20

Go and
See the Wicked Things

I have never written anything about the prophet Ezekiel, nor have I ever preached a message about him. His book has not been a focus of study or attention for me over the years. In fact, I realized as I wrote this chapter that I have purposely avoided Ezekiel. He always seemed so eccentric, the epitome of the Old Testament prophet, and I was afraid I would not understand what I read if I dug into him and his story too deeply. All that will change as we take the next step in our *Go and Obey* journey.

In Ezekiel 8, Ezekiel saw the Lord, "his waist down he was like fire, and from there up his appearance was as bright as glowing metal" (8:2), who "stretched out what looked like a hand and took me by the hair of my head" (8:3), and instructed Ezekiel to "go in and see the wicked and detestable things they are doing here" (8:9). Then in the verse 12, Ezekiel witnessed the elders and leaders of Israel doing abominable things offensive to God. It was so bad that the Lord later said, "Therefore I will deal with them in anger; I will not look on them with pity or spare them. Although they shout in my ears, I will not listen to them" (Ezekiel 8:18). Why would the Lord tell Ezekiel to go and see the wicked things even though the Lord was angry with His people? I'm glad you asked, but to find out, you will have to read on.

FACING REALITY

God would not allow Ezekiel to be His prophet in isolation. Ezekiel could not be a hermit or go into hiding to protect himself from the messy situation his nation was experiencing. He had to face the reality of his peoples' depravity and evil, and see them like God saw them as the abomination they had become. Even the leaders had abandoned their oaths of obedience and were carrying out secret, sinful practices they believed no one saw, not even the Lord. This reminds me of what Jesus prayed for His disciples:

> "I am coming to you now, but I say these things while I am still in the world, so that they may have the full measure of my joy within them. I have given them your word and the world has hated them, for they are not of the world any more than I am of the world. My prayer is not that you take them out of the world but that you protect them from the evil one. They are not of the world, even as I am not of it. Sanctify them by the truth; your word is truth. As you sent me into the world, I have sent them into the world. For them I sanctify myself, that they too may be truly sanctified" (John 17:13–19).

The world can be a nasty place, but we must balance on the tightrope of living in the world while not becoming like the world. God would not allow Ezekiel to look away or ignore the reality of God's fallen creation. He will not allow you to ignore the condition of the world either.

THE LESSONS

We in the church tend to desire a nice, safe, predictable place where we can withdraw from the world. We have done so under the guise of staying holy and pure, but when we withdraw from the world, we deprive the world of any hope of escape from their depraved dilemma. We must follow in the footsteps of Joseph, Daniel, David, Ezekiel, Jeremiah, Paul, and even Jesus Himself, who were all holy but got involved in the unclean business of human existence.

God wants you to express your purpose in churches that have abandoned their role as salt and leaven, in businesses that serve not much more than profit, in government that is looking to use God and His people for their own purposes, and in causes saturated with selfishness and greed. As you immerse yourself in these entities, you cannot become more loyal to them than you are to Him. In other words, you will have to face their abominable practices while you serve them at God's behest. They will want your obedience and fealty, but you cannot give either while you serve them, as Daniel and his friends did with Nebuchadnezzar.

You will fulfill your purpose as Timothy did, among imperfect people who argued and practiced evil as a hobby. Paul's instructions to him are the same instructions the Lord gives you today:

> And the Lord's servant must not be quarrelsome
> but must be kind to everyone, able to teach, not
> resentful. Opponents must be gently instructed,

in the hope that God will grant them repentance leading them to a knowledge of the truth, and that they will come to their senses and escape from the trap of the devil, who has taken them captive to do his will (2 Timothy 2:24–26).

May God grant you grace and wisdom as you serve a holy God in an unholy society.

Chapter 21

Go and
Do not Hesitate

This chapter focuses on the story of Peter's call to go to the Gentiles in Acts 10. Peter was praying on the roof as he waited for his meal and had a vision of a sheet being lowered with all kinds of unclean animals in it. He was commanded to eat, which he refused to do because he kept a kosher diet, and this is what the Spirit said to him:

> While Peter was wondering about the meaning of the vision, the men sent by Cornelius found out where Simon's house was and stopped at the gate. They called out, asking if Simon who was known as Peter was staying there. While Peter was still thinking about the vision, the Spirit said to him, "Simon, three men are looking for you. So get up **and go** downstairs. Do not hesitate to **go** with them, for I have sent them" (Acts 10:17-20, emphasis added).

Let's unpack these verses to see what we can add to our growing understanding of what God wants us to be going to do.

STOP PRAYING AND MEDITATING

Peter went up on the roof to have a quiet time with

the Lord. The Lord interrupted his devotions to impart the next phase of his ministry purpose Jesus had introduced in Matthew 16:

> "Blessed are you, Simon son of Jonah, for this was not revealed to you by flesh and blood, but by my Father in heaven. And I tell you that you are Peter, and on this rock I will build my church, and the gates of Hades will not overcome it. I will give you the keys of the kingdom of heaven; whatever you bind on earth will be bound in heaven, and whatever you loose on earth will be loosed in heaven" (Matthew 16:17-19).

Peter had the keys to the Kingdom and he had to go to the Gentiles to open the Kingdom door for them. The problem was that Peter didn't want to go. He was a good Jew and even though Jesus had personally told him and his comrades to go, they were still hanging around Jerusalem and its environs as good Jews who did not like the Gentiles. The Gentiles were unclean, had strange customs, ate foods forbidden by the Law, and were idolaters—not to mention Judah's military overlords.

God told Peter to leave his comfortable rooftop perch and without hesitation accompany the men who had come to lead him to Cornelius' home. God was not interested in Peter's prayers or his solitude. God was interested in the gospel reaching the Gentiles and it was to start with Cornelius, and Peter had to be the one to go.

THE LESSONS

All my life, I have watched believers retreat into the comfort and safety of their "prayer closets." As a Catholic,

I had a relative who was a Franciscan priest and thus had regular contact with monks who were priests or "brothers." Then when I found the Lord, I ran into many people who defined their ministries as "intercessors." These folks prayed alone while others conducted prayer walks with others or solo, and why wouldn't they?

The prayer closet is quiet and secure. The environment in the prayer closet can be controlled by the one praying. It is a place of study and solitude, meditation and reflection. The problem is that many of these intercessors never came out of their closet, except to refresh and retool to go back in again. There was no messiness of interaction with others and no danger of the prayer agenda being interrupted—except by the Lord. It is all too easy to block out the Lord in the very place we have gone to meet Him, however, as Peter did in this story. God was telling him to do something and Peter said no three times. There are two words that never go together and those words are *Lord* and *no*. If the Lord is beckoning, the response is always yes.

Are you on the rooftop praying? Is God interrupting your alone time and asking you to **go**? **Go** write a book, **go** take a missions trip, **go** back to school, **go** volunteer to help the homeless or youth or the elderly? When you sense any of those, do you run down the stairs from your rooftop perch or do you return the next day and the next and the next, waiting for confirmation or for the Lord to reveal more than He already has? I encourage you to **go** to your closet but when you sense the Lord speaking, say what Eli taught Samuel to say in a similar situation: "Speak, for your servant is listening" (1 Samuel 3:10b). Then when He speaks—and God is always ready to reveal His will if you are listening—get up, go downstairs, and allow others to lead you to the purpose God has for you. Prayer is good, but it should never be used as a delay tactic to keep you from doing what you are praying about doing. Now say your prayers—and then get going!

Chapter 22

Go and Bear Fruit

As we were going to press, I was preaching in my local church and reading from John 15:16: "You did not choose me, but I chose you and appointed you so that you might go and bear fruit—fruit that will last—and so that whatever you ask in my name the Father will give you." As I was reading, I noticed those two magic words—go and—and realized I had missed a verse in my original *Monday Memo* series. As we close this book, let's add this chapter that looks at the concept of spiritual fruit.

FRUIT

God requires His people to be more than nice and polite. He wants them to produce something from their relationship with Him that is unique to who He created them to be. The Bible does not specifically define what fruit is, but we get an indication by considering some of the things written below, such as:

> "For we are God's handiwork, created in Christ Jesus to do good works, which God prepared in advance for us to do" (Ephesians 2:10).

> "For whoever has will be given more, and they will have an abundance. Whoever does not have,

even what they have will be taken from them"
(Matthew 25:29).

"The fruit of the righteous is a tree of life, and
the one who is wise saves lives" (Proverbs 11:30).

"But the fruit of the Spirit is love, joy, peace, for-
bearance, kindness, goodness, faithfulness, gen-
tleness and self-control" (Galatians 5:22-23).

The last passage describes the fruit of the Spirit,
which is not really fruit the believer produces but rather
fruit the Spirit produces in the life of the believer. I include
it because that is the response I most often receive when
I ask people, "What's your fruit?" Therefore, let's not focus
on Galatians 5, but rather on the other verses, which seem
to define fruit as things we say or do, which God expects
us to do more and more.

A DEFINITION

I spent some time reading what others have written
about fruit and one thing is certain: Most people have described what fruit is like but they are hesitant to say what
we should be looking for in our lives that can be called
fruit. Some say that it is souls saved or people we lead to
the Lord. Yet, if truth be told, most people do not lead
many people to the Lord, so does that mean they are not
fruitful? Others say it is a vibrant prayer life, but is fruit defined as the number of prayers a believer says in his or her
lifetime? Finally, some identify fruit as correct doctrine, but
that makes fruit an intellectual pursuit.

Therefore, below I offer my definition of Kingdom
fruit, and challenge you to identify what this fruit is in your
life. Once you identify it (or if you already know what it

is), then I challenge you to determine how you can be even more fruitful. But first, here is my definition:

> *following your joy as you combine your God-given gifts, creativity, purpose, experience, interests, and sustained effort in a way that produces something of value for the benefit of others and yourself.*

My fruit is comprised of the books I write; the libraries I have established in Kenya; the classes I have taught at university; the devotionals I have written, published, and posted on social media for 18 years; and the seminars I have conducted on purpose and creativity. Oh yes, and as the Spirit has produced His fruit in my life, it has translated into tangible expressions of empathy for others in painful and difficult situations to which I formerly paid little attention.

Let me close with this thought: All fruit is measurable and measured. We speak of fruit as a cluster, a bunch, peck, half-bushel, bushel, peck, quart, pound, kilo, acre, or hectare. Therefore, I assume that your fruit, even though it's spiritual, must be measurable as well. This week, spend some time praying and thinking about the question, "What is my fruit?", follow the answer up with another question, "How do I measure it?", and then close with "How can I produce more of it?". If you persevere in seeking the answers, you will bear the fruit of the Kingdom in your life that God expects and enjoys.

Chapter 23

Go and
Make Disciples

For this final entry, let's look at Jesus' last words found in Matthew 28:18-20:

> "All authority in heaven and on earth has been given to me. Therefore **go and** make disciples of all nations, baptizing them in the name of the Father and of the Son and of the Holy Spirit, and teaching them to obey everything I have commanded you. And surely I am with you always, to the very end of the age" (emphasis added).

I thought I would do a point-by-point presentation for this last chapter, so let's see what we can learn from these famous words regularly referred to as the Great Commission.

WHAT PART OF *GO* DON'T YOU UNDERSTAND?

Go is a two-letter word that has serious implications for each of us. Go implies motion, leaving where we are and heading someplace else. Go is open-ended, for we may go across the street or 2,000 miles away. Go is a command without any other specific instructions, which indicates we are expected to figure it out along the way. Go ushers in change that may involve new relationships, assignments, or scenery. The disciples heard these words from Jesus Himself, yet they did not go, lingering in Jerusalem's comfort zone for many years. Some were never able to overcome their bias against Gentiles and their preference for Jewish home cooking and culture, so they stayed—until persecution and divine intervention forced them to go.

Here are some things to consider about this Commission called Great:

1. Jesus has the authority to send you to do whatever He chooses. God will not apologize for what He asks you to do. It is a privilege to serve Him, but it is important to do so willingly. God is not interested in hostages or slaves; He wants volunteers. Will you volunteer to *Go and Obey*? Or is fear causing you to shrink back?

2. Jesus expects His followers to make other disciples. He did not say, "You go and I will make disciples." You may want God to initiate, direct, supervise, develop, and empower your purpose, for it's safer and less risky if you put the onus of going and obeying on Jesus. You are then simply along for the ride. That is not what *Go and Obey* represents. I have worked to make purpose disciples since 1991. It's what I teach and why I write and publish. What is your strategy to impact, train, and raise up others to do what you do or see what you see?

3. Jesus commands you to overcome any bias you have for other people groups. That means

the world is your stage, as Shakespeare wrote. That is a scary proposition and may mean you must abandon the safety of your shoreline for foreign ports of call, or at least places in your own country you would not usually frequent. I often see people act out this prayer: "God, I'll do *whatever* you want me to do—as long as it's in my country, in my state, in my area, with my people, in my town, in my church, on my street, on Sundays from 7 to 9 or Wednesday from 4 to 6, and as long as my child doesn't have a recital or I don't have to work overtime. But God, You know I will do *whatever* it is You want me to do." If you put restrictions and limitations on God's will, don't be surprised if He is not moving in your life or using you for His purpose. When that happens, you can settle for being a good church member, doing God a favor when you attend and even give some money

4. Jesus wants you to take what He teaches you and find a way to share it with others around the world. That is one reason why the internet is so exciting to me. It is something God wants us to use to disseminate His will and teaching, giving us all an outlet for our testimonies, which will help us and others overcome the evil one.

5. Jesus promised that He would be with you no matter where you went or what you did. You are in partnership with God. Be careful,

however, and keep in mind Paul's admoni-
tion: "As God's co-workers we urge you not
to receive God's grace in vain. For he says, 'In
the time of my favor I heard you, and in the
day of salvation I helped you.' I tell you, now
is the time of God's favor, now is the day of
salvation" (2 Corinthians 6:1-2).

There you have it. We have looked at 22 examples
of God's commands that included the words "go and." I
hope I have created an urgency in you to be obedient and
active as you find and express your purpose and creativity.
You are God's hands and feet, and if you don't *Go and Obey*,
then no one will *Go and Obey*. The good news is that Jesus
goes with you when you go, but does that mean He does
not stay with you when you stay? That's a scary thought, so
I will continue to *Go and Obey* as best I can, taking Jesus at
His word that He will never leave or forsake me to the end
of the age. I hope to see you along the *Go and Obey* road.

The Fear Factor

Did you really think we were finished with the *Go and Obey* theme? We are, but I needed to write this epilogue to put the icing on the cake of our discussion. *Go and Obey* has emphasized God's bias for action, but this final thought will focus on mankind's resistance to that call to step out and do whatever it is God has spoken or revealed. The refusal to go is usually rooted in fear, and that is why I have titled this Epilogue "The Fear Factor."

THE REFUSALS

I can think of three situations in which people refused when God told them to go. The first was Jonah, the reluctant prophet, who was told to go to Nineveh and deliver a hard word that God's judgment was coming. Instead of heading to Nineveh, Jonah got on a ship and went in the opposite direction. He eventually revealed that he didn't want to go because he knew the Lord would relent of His verdict if the people repented—which they did and He did. Jonah ended up going, but it was through the whale express that transported him to a spot within walking distance of his assigned destination.

The second refusal was on the part of the apostles. They heard Jesus' word to go, which we looked at in the previous chapter. The apostles, a title which means "sent forth one," chose to stay in their Jerusalem comfort zone. It took persecution for them to get up and go. They prove it is no guarantee that we will go just because we have heard from the Lord, something that many people claim to be true: "If only God would speak to me, *then* I would know, go, and do His will."

Jonah was afraid God would change His mind, and Jonah wanted Nineveh, the enemies of his people, to be wiped out. The apostles were afraid of what their fellow Jews would say when they went to the Gentiles, so they did not go, even with their marching orders in hand. The most significant refusal, however, is found in the Old Testament and we can learn important lessons by examining it more closely.

A TOWER AND A CITY

The Lord told Adam and Eve, and then Noah, to be fruitful and fill the earth. God wanted them to go and spread out, but their descendants rebelled and stayed put. In Genesis 11, we read that the people decided to make a name for themselves, so they settled down to build a monument or tower to give themselves an identity and place they could call their own. What did the Lord do when they refused to go? First, he confused their language and then,

> The Lord scattered them from there over all the earth, and they stopped building the city. That is why it was called Babel—because there the Lord confused the language of the whole world. From there the Lord scattered them over the face of the whole earth (Genesis 11:8-9).

This refusal to go was revisited and reversed at Pentecost in Acts 2 when God once again intervened, this time to give mankind a language of the Spirit that would restore their ability to *Go and Obey* God. As they went, the Spirit would this time aid their communication as evidenced by every man present in Acts 2 hearing God being extolled in their native tongue. Whereas before, God had confused their language in Genesis 11, this time He would clarify it so they could overcome a major barrier to going, which was the inability to communicate.

The people who built the tower were afraid. They were afraid to go out for whatever reason. Perhaps they were afraid they would lose their identity. Maybe they were fearful of what they would find as they went. They were willing to make bricks in the desert, adding heat to an already unbearable climate, just so they would not have to go.

Are you doing the same thing? Are you making bricks in the desert with people you don't understand (and who don't understand you)? Has God confused the communication between you and others because you are in the wrong place? Is all this rooted in the fear factor that if you go, you will somehow lose something instead of gain? When I say go, it doesn't mean you must go far away (although you may). It does mean, however, that you must be in motion to take the initiative concerning what God has put in your heart to do. Where is the fear factor keeping you from going and obeying?

As we close this book, I advise you to consider where you are and where God wants you to be. If they are not the same, then right now your work and way are probably hard. If you go, whether it's to go and write, go and speak, go and learn, go and build, go and proclaim, or go and create, then God will go with you and you will experience the true power of Pentecost. You will sense God's help and it will be exhilarating. Your message will be clear because you are clear. May the Lord reveal to you what your *Go and Obey* is, and then may you face and overcome your fear, knowing that He will be with you to the ends of the earth—or to the end of your street, wherever it is He has chosen for you to serve.

About the Author

John Stanko was born in Pittsburgh, Pennsylvania. After graduating from St. Basil's Prep School in Stamford, Connecticut, he attended Duquesne University where he received his bachelor's and master's degrees in economics in 1972 and 1974 respectively.

Since then, John has served as an administrator, teacher, consultant, author, and pastor in his profession-al career. He holds a second master's degree in pastoral min-istries, and earned his doctorate in pastoral ministries from Liberty Theological Seminary in Houston, Texas in 1995. He recently completed a second doctor of ministry degree at Reformed Presbyterian Theological Seminary in Pittsburgh.

John has taught extensively on the topics of time management, life purpose and organization, and has con-ducted leadership and purpose training sessions throughout the United States and in 32 countries. He is also certified to administer the DISC and other related personality assess-ments as well as the Natural Church Development profile for churches. In 2006, he earned the privilege to facilitate for The Pacific Institute of Seattle, a leadership and person-al development program, and for The Leadership Circle, a provider of cultural and executive 360-degree profiles. He has authored fifteen books and written for many publica-tions around the world.

John founded a personal and leadership development

company, called PurposeQuest, in 2001 and today travels the world to speak, consult and inspire leaders and people everywhere. From 2001-2008, he spent six months a year in Africa and still enjoys visiting and working on that continent, while teaching for Geneva College's Masters of Organizational Leadership and the Center for Urban Biblical Ministry in his hometown of Pittsburgh, Pennsylvania. John has been married for 44 years to Kathryn Scimone Stanko, and they have two adult children. In 2009, John was appointed the administrative pastor for discipleship at Allegheny Center Alliance Church on the North Side of Pittsburgh where he served for five years. Most recently, John founded Urban Press, a publishing service designed to tell stories of the city, from the city, and to the city.

Keep in Touch
with
John W. Stanko

www.purposequest.com
www.johnstanko.us
www.stankobiblestudy.com
www.stankomondaymemo.com
or via email at johnstanko@gmail.com

John also does extensive relief and community development work in Kenya. You can see some of his projects at www.purposequest.com/contributions

PurposeQuest International
PO Box 8882
Pittsburgh, PA 15221-0882

Additional Titles by John W. Stanko

A Daily Dose of Proverbs
A Daily Taste of Proverbs
Changing the Way We Do Church
I Wrote This Book on Purpose
Life Is A Gold Mine: Can You Dig It?
Strictly Business
The Faith Files, Volume 1
The Faith Files, Volume 2
The Faith Files, Volume 3
The Leadership Walk
The Price of Leadership
Unlocking the Power of Your Creativity
Unlocking the Power of Your Productivity
Unlocking the Power of Your Purpose
Unlocking the Power of You
What Would Jesus Ask You Today?
Your Life Matters

Live the Word Commentary: Matthew
Live the Word Commentary: Mark
Live the Word Commentary: Luke
Live the Word Commentary: John
Live the Word Commentary: Acts
Live the Word Commentary: Romans
Live the Word Commentary: Galatians, Ephesians,
Philippians, Colossians, Philemon
Live the Word Commentary: Revelation

www.ingramcontent.com/pod-product-compliance
Lightning Source LLC
Chambersburg PA
CBHW072041040426
42447CB00012BB/2961